I0446339

MASTERING

INTRADAY TRADING

Proven Strategies for Success

by

Lalit Mohanty

Table of Contents

- Understanding Intraday Trading

- Risks and Rewards

- Key Terminology

Chapter 2: Setting Up Your Intraday Trading Workspace

- Choosing the Right Trading Platform

- Technical Analysis Tools

- Real-time Data Feeds

Chapter 3: Strategy 1 - Momentum Trading

- Identifying Momentum Stocks

- Using Moving Averages

- RSI (Relative Strength Index) Strategies

Chapter 4: Strategy 2 - Gap Trading

- Recognizing Gap Opportunities

- Fading or Riding the Gap

- Risk Management in Gap Trading

Chapter 5: Strategy 3 - Breakout Trading

- Spotting Breakout Opportunities
- Trading the Opening Range Breakout
- Volume Confirmation in Breakouts

Chapter 6: Strategy 4 - Reversal Trading

- Identifying Trend Reversals
- Candlestick Patterns for Reversals
- Trading Divergences

Chapter 7: Strategy 5 - Scalping

- Overview of Scalping
- Key Indicators for Scalping
- Risk Management in Scalping

Chapter 8: Strategy 6 - Mean Reversion Trading

- Understanding Mean Reversion
- Bollinger Bands and Mean Reversion
- Trading Ranges and Mean Reversion

Chapter 9: Strategy 7 - News-Based Trading

- Incorporating News into Your Strategy

- Reacting to Economic Indicators

- Earnings Reports and Trading Opportunities

Chapter 10: Strategy 8 - Algorithmic Trading

- Introduction to Algorithmic Trading

- Developing Simple Algorithms

- Risks and Considerations in Algorithmic Trading

Chapter 11: Risk Management Techniques

- Position Sizing

- Setting Stop-Loss Orders

- Diversification in Intraday Trading

Chapter 12: Psychology of Intraday Trading

- Managing Emotions

- Discipline and Patience

- Learning from Losses

Chapter 13: Record-Keeping and Analysis

- Importance of Keeping a Trading Journal
- Analyzing Trade Performance
- Continuous Learning and Improvement

Chapter 14: Putting It All Together - Creating Your Intraday Trading Plan

- Building a Personalized Trading Plan
- Testing and Adjusting Strategies
- Setting Realistic Goals

Chapter 15: Advanced Intraday Trading Techniques

- Options Trading Strategies
- Trading during Economic Events
- Global Market Considerations

Conclusion: Mastering the Art of Intraday Trading

Appendix: Resources for Intraday Traders

- Recommended Books

- Online Courses

- Trading Communities

Lalit Prasad Mohanty

PREFACE

This book is designed to provide a comprehensive guide to intraday trading strategies, covering a range of techniques suitable for different market conditions and trader preferences. Each chapter offers practical insights, real-world examples, and actionable tips to help readers develop their own successful intraday trading approach.

CHAPTER 1

INTRODUCTION TO INTRADAY TRADING

Intraday trading, often referred to as day trading, is a financial strategy where traders buy and sell financial instruments within the same trading day. Unlike long-term investing, which involves holding onto assets for an extended period, intraday traders aim to capitalize on short-term price movements to generate profits. This chapter provides an in-depth introduction to the world of intraday trading, covering its basics, risks, rewards, and essential terminology.

Understanding Intraday Trading

Intraday trading operates on the principle of capturing small price fluctuations within a single trading day. Traders seek to leverage market volatility, profiting from the price differences between buying and selling assets over short time frames. This approach demands quick decision-making, a keen understanding of market trends, and the ability to manage risks effectively.

Successful intraday traders often rely on technical analysis, studying price charts, patterns, and various indicators to make informed trading decisions. Timing is critical, and traders must be adept at executing orders swiftly to take advantage of fleeting opportunities.

Risks and Rewards

Intraday trading offers both significant rewards and inherent risks. The potential for quick profits attracts many traders, but the volatility that facilitates these gains also exposes them to substantial risks. Market fluctuations can occur rapidly, leading to both profitable and losing trades within short time intervals.

Risk management is paramount in intraday trading. Traders must establish clear risk-reward ratios, set stop-loss orders to limit potential losses, and avoid overleveraging their positions. Understanding and mitigating risks are fundamental aspects of sustainable intraday trading strategies.

Key Terminology

To navigate the intricacies of intraday trading, it's crucial to familiarize oneself with key terminology. Here are some essential terms to grasp:

1. **Bid and Ask Prices:** The bid price represents what buyers are willing to pay, while the ask price is the amount sellers are asking for the asset.

2. **Spread:** The difference between the bid and ask prices.

3. **Liquidity:** The ease with which an asset can be bought or sold without affecting its price.

4. **Volatility:** The degree of variation in an asset's price over time.

5. **Leverage:** Using borrowed capital to increase the size of a trading position.

6. **Short Selling:** Selling an asset with the expectation of buying it back later at a lower price.

7. **Candlestick Charts:** Visual representations of price movements, displaying open, high, low, and close prices.

8. **Moving Averages:** A statistical calculation used to analyze data points over a specific period, helping identify trends.

By understanding and employing these terms, traders can communicate effectively, interpret market information, and make informed decisions in the fast-paced world of intraday trading.

In conclusion, intraday trading is a dynamic and challenging approach to the financial markets. This chapter has provided a foundation for understanding the principles, risks, and rewards associated with intraday trading, laying the groundwork for exploring specific strategies in the chapters that follow.

CHAPTER 2

SETTING UP YOUR INTRADAY TRADING WORKSPACE

Setting up an effective intraday trading workspace is crucial for success in the fast-paced world of day trading. In this chapter, we will delve into the essential elements that make up an efficient trading environment, including selecting the right trading platform, utilizing technical analysis tools, and ensuring access to real-time data feeds.

Choosing the Right Trading Platform

Selecting an appropriate trading platform is a critical decision for intraday traders. The platform serves as the interface between the trader and the financial markets, facilitating the execution of trades and providing essential market information. Consider the following factors when choosing a trading platform:

1. **Execution Speed:** In intraday trading, every second counts. Opt for a platform with rapid order execution to ensure that your trades are executed promptly at the desired prices.

2. **User Interface:** Choose a platform with an intuitive and user-friendly interface. A clean and well-organized layout can enhance your ability to monitor market conditions and execute trades efficiently.

3. **Charting Features:** Robust charting tools are essential for technical analysis. Look for a platform that offers a variety of chart types, timeframes, and technical indicators to support your analysis.

4. **Order Types:** Ensure that the platform supports a range of order types, including market orders, limit orders, and stop orders. This flexibility allows you to implement different trading strategies.

5. **Reliability:** A stable and reliable platform is crucial for intraday trading. Downtime or technical glitches can result in missed opportunities and financial losses.

6. **Costs and Fees:** Consider the cost structure of the platform, including commissions, fees, and margin rates. Be aware of any additional costs that may impact your overall profitability.

Research and trial different platforms before committing to one. Many brokers offer demo accounts, allowing you to test the platform's features and functionality without risking real capital.

Technical Analysis Tools

Technical analysis is a cornerstone of intraday trading, and having the right tools is essential for making informed decisions. Here are key technical analysis tools to include in your intraday trading workspace:

1. **Candlestick Charts:** Provide visual representations of price movements, offering insights into market sentiment and potential trends.

2. **Moving Averages:** Smooth out price data to identify trends and reversals over specific time periods.

3. **RSI (Relative Strength Index):** Measures the magnitude of recent price changes, helping identify overbought or oversold conditions.

4. **Bollinger Bands:** Display price volatility and potential reversal points based on standard deviations from a moving average.

5. **MACD (Moving Average Convergence Divergence):** Highlights changes in momentum, useful for identifying trend reversals.

Customize your charts with the indicators and tools that align with your trading strategy. Regularly update and refine your technical analysis toolkit as you gain experience and adapt to changing market conditions.

Real-time Data Feeds

Access to real-time market data is imperative for intraday traders who need up-to-the-second information to make timely decisions. Consider the following aspects when evaluating real-time data feeds:

1. **Market Coverage:** Ensure that the data feed covers the financial instruments you intend to trade, including stocks, forex pairs, commodities, and indices.

2. **Data Accuracy:** Reliable and accurate data is crucial for making informed trading decisions. Choose a data provider with a reputation for delivering precise market information.

3. **Latency:** Minimize latency in data delivery to receive timely updates. A delay in data can impact your ability to react quickly to changing market conditions.

4. **Cost:** Evaluate the cost of subscribing to real-time data feeds, considering your budget and the value they add to your trading strategy.

5. **Integration with Trading Platform:** Confirm that the data feed seamlessly integrates with your chosen trading platform, ensuring smooth data transmission and execution of trades.

By establishing a trading workspace with the right platform, technical analysis tools, and real-time data feeds, you set the foundation for executing effective intraday trading strategies. In the subsequent chapters, we will explore specific intraday trading strategies that leverage these tools to capitalize on short-term market movements.

CHAPTER 3

STRATEGY 1 - MOMENTUM TRADING

Momentum trading is a popular intraday strategy that capitalizes on the continuation of existing price trends. Traders employing momentum strategies aim to ride the wave of accelerating price movements and capture profits as trends develop. This chapter explores the key components of momentum trading, including identifying momentum stocks, utilizing moving averages, and implementing strategies based on the Relative Strength Index (RSI).

Identifying Momentum Stocks

Successful momentum trading begins with the identification of stocks exhibiting strong price momentum. Here are some key factors to consider when identifying momentum stocks:

1. **Price Trends:** Look for stocks with clear and sustained price trends. A strong uptrend indicates buying momentum, while a downtrend signals selling pressure.

2. **Volume Confirmation:** Verify that the price movement is supported by significant trading volume. Volume confirms the strength of the price trend, indicating active participation from buyers or sellers.

3. **News Catalysts:** Explore recent news and events that could be driving the stock's momentum. Positive news, such as earnings reports or product launches, can fuel upward momentum, while negative news may lead to downward momentum.

4. **Sector Strength:** Consider the overall strength of the sector to which the stock belongs. Stocks within a strong sector are more likely to exhibit sustained momentum.

5. **Relative Strength Comparison:** Compare the stock's performance to relevant benchmarks or indices. A stock outperforming its peers or the broader market may have strong momentum.

Using Moving Averages

Moving averages are essential tools for momentum traders, providing a smoothed representation of price trends over specific time periods. Here's how to use moving averages in momentum trading:

1. **Simple Moving Averages (SMA):** Identify the overall trend direction by using SMAs with different timeframes. A shorter-term SMA (e.g., 50 days) reacts quickly to price changes, while a longer-term SMA (e.g., 200 days) provides a broader perspective.

2. **Golden Cross and Death Cross:** Look for "Golden Cross" patterns, where the shorter-term SMA crosses above the longer-term SMA, signaling a potential uptrend. Conversely, a "Death Cross" occurs when the shorter-term SMA crosses below the longer-term SMA, suggesting a potential downtrend.

3. **Moving Average Crossovers:** Monitor crossovers between the price and its moving averages. When the price crosses above the moving average, it may indicate bullish momentum, while a crossover below could suggest bearish momentum.

RSI (Relative Strength Index) Strategies

The Relative Strength Index (RSI) is a momentum oscillator that measures the speed and change of price movements. It ranges from 0 to 100 and is used to identify overbought or oversold conditions. Here's how to integrate RSI into momentum trading strategies:

1. **Overbought and Oversold Conditions:** RSI values above 70 indicate overbought conditions, suggesting a potential reversal or pullback. Conversely, RSI values below 30 indicate oversold conditions, signaling a potential buying opportunity.

2. **Divergence:** Look for divergence between RSI and price movements. If the price is making new highs,

but the RSI is not, it could indicate weakening momentum, potentially leading to a reversal.

3. **RSI Trendline Breaks:** Draw trendlines on the RSI chart and observe breaks. If the RSI breaks above a downtrend line, it may signal a potential bullish momentum shift, and vice versa.

In conclusion, momentum trading is a dynamic strategy that involves identifying and capitalizing on stocks with strong price trends. By combining the identification of momentum stocks, the use of moving averages, and incorporating RSI strategies, traders can develop a robust approach to capturing short-term price movements. As we progress through this guide, we'll explore additional intraday trading strategies, each offering unique insights and techniques for navigating the financial markets.

CHAPTER 4

STRATEGY 2 - GAP TRADING

Gap trading is an intraday strategy that capitalizes on price gaps between the closing price of the previous day and the opening price of the current day. Gaps often occur due to overnight news or events, creating opportunities for traders to profit from the subsequent price movement. This chapter explores the fundamentals of gap trading, including recognizing gap opportunities, deciding whether to fade or ride the gap, and implementing effective risk management.

Recognizing Gap Opportunities

Gaps can be classified into three main types:

1. **Common Gap:** A gap that does not signify a significant change in the trend and is likely to be filled relatively quickly.

2. **Breakaway Gap:** Occurs when a stock gaps above a significant resistance level, suggesting a potential change in trend or the beginning of a new trend.

3. **Exhaustion Gap:** Appears near the end of a trend, indicating a final attempt to continue the trend before a reversal.

To recognize gap opportunities, traders should use pre-market scanners or gap-up/gap-down lists to identify stocks with substantial overnight price changes. Additionally, news sources and corporate announcements can provide insights into the reasons behind the gaps.

Fading or Riding the Gap

Gap traders can choose between two primary approaches: fading the gap or riding the gap.

1. **Fading the Gap:** This strategy involves betting on the price reverting to its previous day's closing level. Traders anticipate that the initial gap will be filled as the price retraces, either partially or entirely. Fading the gap requires close monitoring of price action and the use of appropriate technical indicators to confirm potential reversals.

2. **Riding the Gap:** Traders who opt to ride the gap aim to capitalize on the continuation of the gap's direction. If the gap is in the direction of the prevailing trend, traders may choose to enter a position in the hope of further price movement in that direction. Technical analysis tools, such as trendlines and moving

averages, can assist in identifying the strength of the trend.

Risk Management in Gap Trading

Effective risk management is crucial in gap trading to mitigate potential losses. Consider the following risk management principles:

1. **Setting Stop-Loss Orders:** Determine a predetermined point at which you will exit the trade to limit losses. This point can be based on a percentage of the gap size or a specific technical level.

2. **Position Sizing:** Adjust the size of your position based on the size of the gap and your risk tolerance. Smaller position sizes can help manage risk in volatile conditions.

3. **Time Management:** Gap trades often unfold quickly, so be prepared to act promptly. Set time-based exit criteria to avoid holding positions for an extended period if the expected price movement does not materialize.

4. **Diversification:** Avoid overconcentration in a single gap trade. Diversifying your trades across different stocks or assets can help spread risk.

5. **Monitoring News and Events:** Stay informed about potential news or events that may impact the gap

trade. Unexpected developments can influence price movements and affect your risk exposure.

In conclusion, gap trading offers unique opportunities for intraday traders to profit from overnight price gaps. Recognizing gap opportunities, deciding whether to fade or ride the gap, and implementing effective risk management are key elements of a successful gap trading strategy. As we progress through this guide, we will explore additional intraday trading strategies, each providing valuable insights and techniques for navigating the dynamic landscape of intraday trading.

CHAPTER 5

STRATEGY 3 - BREAKOUT TRADING

Breakout trading is a strategy that focuses on identifying key levels of support or resistance and capitalizing on significant price movements that occur when these levels are breached. This chapter explores the essentials of breakout trading, including spotting breakout opportunities, trading the opening range breakout, and understanding the importance of volume confirmation in breakout strategies.

Spotting Breakout Opportunities

Breakouts occur when an asset's price moves beyond a well-defined level of support or resistance. Traders aim to identify breakout opportunities by analyzing chart patterns and key technical levels. Common breakout patterns include:

1. **Triangles:** Ascending, descending, or symmetrical triangles can signal potential breakouts.

2. **Rectangles:** Consolidation patterns with horizontal support and resistance lines often precede breakouts.

3. **Channels:** Trading within upward or downward channels may result in breakouts when the price reaches the channel boundaries.

4. **Head and Shoulders:** This reversal pattern can also act as a continuation pattern, leading to breakouts in the direction of the prevailing trend.

Traders use technical indicators, trendlines, and chart patterns to confirm potential breakout opportunities and make informed entry decisions.

Trading the Opening Range Breakout

The opening range breakout is a specific variation of breakout trading that focuses on the price movement during the initial trading period of the day. Here's how to trade the opening range breakout:

1. **Define the Opening Range:** Identify the high and low prices during the initial trading period, typically the first 15 to 30 minutes after the market opens.

2. **Wait for Breakout Confirmation:** Enter a trade when the price breaks above the high or below the low of the opening range. This breakout often signifies the beginning of a trend for the day.

3. **Set Stop-Loss and Take-Profit Levels:** Establish stop-loss orders to manage potential losses and take-profit levels to secure gains. Consider using technical

indicators, such as moving averages or support/resistance levels, to determine these levels.

4. **Volume Confirmation:** Confirm the breakout with an increase in trading volume. Higher volume during a breakout indicates stronger market participation and can enhance the reliability of the breakout.

Volume Confirmation in Breakouts

Volume is a crucial factor in breakout trading, providing confirmation of the strength and sustainability of a price movement. Consider the following aspects of volume confirmation:

1. **Increasing Volume:** A breakout accompanied by a surge in trading volume suggests strong market interest and increases the likelihood of a sustained trend.

2. **Decreasing Volume:** Conversely, a breakout with decreasing volume may indicate weakening momentum and could be a false signal.

3. **Volume Patterns:** Analyze volume patterns, such as volume spikes or clusters, to identify potential turning points or continuation signals.

4. **Compare Volume to Averages:** Compare current trading volume to historical averages for the specific

asset. Significant deviations from the norm can signal unusual market activity.

In conclusion, breakout trading is a dynamic strategy that capitalizes on the potential for significant price movements when key levels of support or resistance are breached. By spotting breakout opportunities, trading the opening range breakout, and incorporating volume confirmation, traders can enhance their ability to identify and capitalize on trends in the intraday market. As we progress through this guide, we will explore additional intraday trading strategies, each providing valuable insights and techniques for navigating the dynamic landscape of intraday trading.

CHAPTER 6

STRATEGY 4 - REVERSAL TRADING

Reversal trading is a strategy that involves identifying potential changes in the prevailing trend and positioning trades to capitalize on these reversals. This chapter explores the key aspects of reversal trading, including techniques for identifying trend reversals, recognizing candlestick patterns indicative of reversals, and utilizing divergence in trading.

Identifying Trend Reversals

Recognizing the early signs of a potential trend reversal is crucial for reversal traders. Here are some key indicators and techniques to identify trend reversals:

1. **Trendline Breaks:** A break below an uptrend line or above a downtrend line may signal a potential reversal.

2. **Support and Resistance Levels:** Observe how price interacts with key support and resistance levels. A breach of a significant level may indicate a reversal.

3. **Moving Averages:** Crossovers or deviations from moving averages can signal changes in trend direction. For example, a stock crossing below its 50-

day moving average after an uptrend may suggest a potential reversal.

4. **Volume Analysis:** An increase in trading volume during a price reversal can provide confirmation of a potential trend change.

5. **Momentum Indicators:** Oscillators like the Relative Strength Index (RSI) or the Moving Average Convergence Divergence (MACD) can signal overbought or oversold conditions, indicating a potential reversal.

Candlestick Patterns for Reversals

Candlestick patterns are powerful tools for identifying potential trend reversals. Some common reversal candlestick patterns include:

1. **Hammer and Hanging Man:** These single-candle patterns indicate potential reversals after a downtrend (hammer) or an uptrend (hanging man).

2. **Engulfing Patterns:** Bullish engulfing and bearish engulfing patterns involve one candle fully engulfing the previous one, signaling potential trend reversals.

3. **Doji:** A doji occurs when the opening and closing prices are virtually the same, suggesting indecision in the market and potential reversals.

4. **Double Tops and Bottoms:** These patterns involve two price peaks (double top) or troughs (double bottom) and suggest potential trend reversals.

5. **Three Inside Up and Three Inside Down:** These three-candle patterns indicate potential reversals, with the third candle closing higher (three inside up) or lower (three inside down) than the previous two.

Trading Divergences

Divergence occurs when the price of an asset moves in the opposite direction of a technical indicator, signaling a potential trend reversal. Common types of divergences include:

1. **Regular Divergence:** Occurs when the price forms a higher high or lower low, while the indicator does not follow suit. This can indicate weakening momentum and a potential reversal.

2. **Hidden Divergence:** Involves the price forming a higher high or lower low, while the indicator forms a lower high or higher low. Hidden divergence may suggest the continuation of the existing trend.

3. **MACD Divergence:** A divergence between the price chart and the MACD histogram can signal potential reversals.

In conclusion, reversal trading is a strategy that requires a keen understanding of market dynamics and the ability to identify early signs of trend changes. By employing techniques such as identifying trend reversals, recognizing candlestick patterns for reversals, and trading divergences, traders can enhance their ability to spot potential reversals and position themselves for profitable trades. As we progress through this guide, we will explore additional intraday trading strategies, each providing valuable insights and techniques for navigating the dynamic landscape of intraday trading.

CHAPTER 7

STRATEGY 5 – SCALPING

Scalping is a short-term trading strategy that aims to capitalize on small price movements within the market. Scalpers seek to make numerous quick trades throughout the day, taking advantage of minor fluctuations in price. This chapter provides a comprehensive overview of scalping, including key indicators for scalping and effective risk management techniques.

Overview of Scalping

Scalping is characterized by its rapid pace and the focus on exploiting very short-term price changes. Scalpers typically hold positions for a few seconds to a few minutes, aiming to accumulate small profits consistently. The key features of scalping include:

1. **Quick Decision-Making:** Scalpers need to make swift decisions based on immediate market conditions and technical signals.

2. **High Trade Frequency:** Scalpers execute a large number of trades within a single day, aiming to generate profits from cumulative small price changes.

3. **Leverage:** Scalping often involves the use of leverage to amplify the potential gains from small price

movements. However, this also increases the risk, requiring careful risk management.

4. **Tight Spreads:** Scalpers benefit from tight bid-ask spreads to minimize costs. They often focus on highly liquid markets and currency pairs.

5. **Technological Tools:** Scalpers rely on advanced trading platforms and technology for quick order execution and access to real-time market data.

Key Indicators for Scalping

Successful scalping requires a combination of technical indicators that provide timely and accurate signals. Here are key indicators commonly used in scalping:

1. **Moving Averages:** Short-term moving averages, such as the 5-period or 10-period, can help identify the immediate trend direction.

2. **Stochastic Oscillator:** This momentum indicator helps identify overbought and oversold conditions, guiding entry and exit points.

3. **Bollinger Bands:** Scalpers use Bollinger Bands to identify volatility and potential reversal points. Price touching the upper or lower band may indicate overextension.

4. **Relative Strength Index (RSI):** The RSI can signal potential reversals and overbought/oversold conditions, aiding in decision-making.

5. **Support and Resistance Levels:** Identifying key support and resistance levels helps scalpers set entry and exit points. Breakouts or bounces from these levels can offer trading opportunities.

6. **Volume Analysis:** Monitoring trading volume is crucial for confirming price movements. A surge in volume during a price change adds credibility to the move.

Risk Management in Scalping

Given the high-frequency nature of scalping, effective risk management is paramount to preserve capital. Here are key principles for managing risk in scalping:

1. **Set Tight Stop-Loss Orders:** Define precise exit points to limit potential losses. Scalpers often use tight stop-loss orders to control risk.

2. **Position Sizing:** Determine the size of each position based on the risk tolerance for the trade. Scalpers may use a fixed percentage of their trading capital for each trade.

3. **Risk-Reward Ratio:** Assess the potential reward relative to the risk before entering a trade. A positive

risk-reward ratio ensures that potential gains outweigh potential losses.

4. **Constant Monitoring:** Scalpers need to monitor positions continuously and be ready to act quickly. Unforeseen market events can occur rapidly, and staying vigilant is essential.

5. **Avoid Overtrading:** While scalping involves frequent trading, overtrading can lead to losses. Stick to a predefined trading plan and only take high-probability setups.

6. **Adapt to Market Conditions:** Scalpers must be adaptable to changing market conditions. If conditions are unfavorable, it's crucial to step back and reassess.

In conclusion, scalping is a dynamic and intense trading strategy that demands quick thinking, precision, and effective risk management. By understanding the overview of scalping, utilizing key indicators, and implementing risk management techniques, traders can enhance their ability to navigate the fast-paced world of short-term trading. As we progress through this guide, we will explore additional intraday trading strategies, each providing valuable insights and techniques for navigating the dynamic landscape of intraday trading.

CHAPTER 8
STRATEGY 6 - MEAN REVERSION TRADING

Mean reversion trading is a strategy based on the belief that asset prices tend to revert to their historical average or mean over time. Traders employing this strategy look for deviations from the mean and anticipate a return to the average. This chapter explores the principles of mean reversion trading, the role of Bollinger Bands in identifying mean reversion opportunities, and how to trade price ranges with a mean reversion approach.

Understanding Mean Reversion

Mean reversion is grounded in the idea that, over time, asset prices fluctuate around a central or average value. This central value can be represented by various metrics, such as a simple moving average or a historical average price. The key concepts of mean reversion trading include:

1. **Overbought and Oversold Conditions:** Mean reversion traders identify instances where an asset is deemed overbought (trading above its average) or oversold (trading below its average). They anticipate a correction toward the mean.

2. **Historical Averages:** Historical averages, such as the 50-day or 200-day moving average, serve as reference points for mean reversion traders. Deviations from these averages may present trading opportunities.

3. **Statistical Measures:** Traders often use statistical measures like standard deviations to quantify how far an asset's price has deviated from its mean. This helps in determining potential entry and exit points.

Bollinger Bands and Mean Reversion

Bollinger Bands, a technical indicator developed by John Bollinger, are widely used in mean reversion trading. These bands consist of a central moving average and upper and lower bands representing standard deviations from the mean. Here's how Bollinger Bands are utilized in mean reversion trading:

1. **Identifying Overbought and Oversold Conditions:** When prices touch or exceed the upper band, it may suggest overbought conditions, and a reversal to the mean could be anticipated. Conversely, prices touching or falling below the lower band might indicate oversold conditions.

2. **Trading the Bands:** Mean reversion traders may initiate trades when prices reach the outer bands, anticipating a return to the mean. Confirmation from other indicators or price action is often sought to increase the reliability of signals.

3. **Volatility Expansion and Contraction:** Bollinger Bands expand during periods of high volatility and contract during low volatility. Mean reversion traders

consider these changes in volatility to time their entries and exits.

Trading Ranges and Mean Reversion

Mean reversion is closely associated with trading within ranges. When an asset is moving within a well-defined range, mean reversion traders look for opportunities at the extremes of the range. Here's how to trade ranges with a mean reversion approach:

1. **Identify Trading Ranges:** Use technical analysis to identify price ranges where the asset has historically moved. Support and resistance levels can serve as boundaries for these ranges.

2. **Wait for Extremes:** Patiently wait for the price to reach the upper or lower bounds of the range. This is when mean reversion traders consider initiating positions.

3. **Use Confirmation Indicators:** Additional indicators, such as oscillators or trendlines, can be used to confirm potential mean reversion opportunities within trading ranges.

4. **Set Realistic Targets:** Mean reversion traders often set conservative profit targets, aiming for a move back toward the range's center rather than expecting a complete reversal.

In conclusion, mean reversion trading is based on the idea that asset prices tend to revert to their historical average over time. By understanding mean reversion principles, utilizing Bollinger Bands, and trading within established ranges, traders can develop effective strategies for identifying and capitalizing on mean reversion opportunities. As we progress through this guide, we will explore additional intraday trading strategies, each providing valuable insights and techniques for navigating the dynamic landscape of intraday trading.

CHAPTER 9

STRATEGY 7 - NEWS-BASED TRADING

News-based trading involves making trading decisions based on the release of relevant news, events, or economic indicators that can impact financial markets. Traders leveraging this strategy aim to capitalize on the rapid market movements and volatility triggered by significant news developments. This chapter explores the fundamentals of incorporating news into your trading strategy, reacting to economic indicators, and seizing trading opportunities presented by earnings reports.

Incorporating News into Your Strategy

Effective news-based trading requires a systematic approach to incorporating information into your strategy. Here are key considerations for integrating news into your trading:

1. **Stay Informed:** Actively follow financial news, economic reports, and geopolitical events that could influence the markets. Utilize reputable news sources, financial websites, and official government releases.

2. **Economic Calendar:** Use an economic calendar to track upcoming releases of economic indicators, central bank statements, and other key events. Economic calendars provide schedules of news releases and their expected impact on the market.

3. **Volatility Analysis:** Anticipate increased market volatility during and after major news events. Adjust your risk management strategy to account for potential price swings.

4. **Market Sentiment:** Understand market sentiment surrounding news events. Traders often react emotionally to news, leading to exaggerated price movements. Gauge sentiment through market analysis and sentiment indicators.

5. **Preparation and Planning:** Plan your trades in advance of news releases. Determine entry and exit points, as well as risk management parameters, to execute trades swiftly when news breaks.

Reacting to Economic Indicators

Economic indicators are key metrics that provide insights into the economic health of a country or region. Traders closely watch these indicators for potential trading opportunities. Common economic indicators include:

1. **Gross Domestic Product (GDP):** Indicates the overall economic performance of a country.

2. **Unemployment Rate:** Reflects the percentage of the workforce that is unemployed.

3. **Consumer Price Index (CPI):** Measures inflation by tracking changes in the prices of a basket of consumer goods and services.

4. **Interest Rates:** Decisions by central banks on interest rates can significantly impact currency values and broader market sentiment.

Traders can react to economic indicators by:

- **Analyzing Expectations:** Compare actual data releases to market expectations. Deviations from expectations can lead to significant market movements.

- **Currency Trading:** Economic indicators often impact currency values. Traders in the forex market may consider currency pairs related to the countries releasing economic data.

- **Sector-Specific Trades:** Economic indicators can influence specific sectors. For example, positive employment data may benefit consumer-related stocks.

Earnings Reports and Trading Opportunities

Earnings reports, released by publicly traded companies, provide insights into their financial health and performance. These reports can create significant trading opportunities. Here's how traders can leverage earnings reports:

1. **Earnings Calendar:** Keep track of earnings release dates using an earnings calendar. This allows for strategic planning around potentially market-moving events.

2. **Volatility Strategies:** Anticipate increased volatility during earnings season. Traders may use options

strategies or adjust position sizes to manage risk effectively.

3. **Analyst Expectations:** Compare actual earnings results to analysts' expectations. A company exceeding or falling short of expectations can lead to price movements.

4. **After-Hours Trading:** Earnings reports are often released outside regular trading hours. Be prepared for after-hours trading if you intend to react immediately to the news.

5. **Sector Rotation:** Earnings reports can influence sector rotation as money moves in and out of industries based on corporate performance.

In conclusion, news-based trading is a dynamic strategy that requires staying informed, reacting swiftly to economic indicators, and capitalizing on trading opportunities presented by earnings reports. By incorporating news into your strategy, you can navigate the fast-paced world of financial markets and make informed decisions based on the latest information. As we progress through this guide, we will explore additional intraday trading strategies, each providing valuable insights and techniques for navigating the dynamic landscape of intraday trading.

CHAPTER 10

STRATEGY 8 - ALGORITHMIC TRADING

Algorithmic trading, often referred to as algo trading or automated trading, involves using computer algorithms to execute trading strategies. This chapter provides an introduction to algorithmic trading, discusses the development of simple algorithms, and explores the risks and considerations associated with this sophisticated form of trading.

Introduction to Algorithmic Trading

Algorithmic trading has become increasingly prevalent in financial markets, driven by advancements in technology and the need for efficiency and speed in executing trades. Key characteristics of algorithmic trading include:

1. **Speed:** Algorithms enable the execution of trades at speeds impossible for manual traders, capitalizing on price discrepancies in fractions of a second.

2. **Precision:** Algorithms can be programmed to execute trades with precision, avoiding the emotional and human errors often associated with manual trading.

3. **Market Analysis:** Algorithms can analyze vast amounts of market data, identify patterns, and execute trades based on predefined criteria.

4. **24/7 Trading:** Algorithms can operate around the clock, taking advantage of opportunities in different time zones and reacting to news and events as they unfold.

5. **Backtesting:** Traders can test algorithms on historical data to assess their performance before deploying them in live markets.

Developing Simple Algorithms

Developing algorithmic trading strategies can range from simple to highly complex. Here's a guide to developing simple algorithms for intraday trading:

1. **Define Objectives:** Clearly outline the objectives of your algorithm. Are you aiming for high-frequency trades, mean reversion, trend following, or a combination?

2. **Select Indicators:** Choose technical indicators suitable for your strategy. Common indicators include moving averages, RSI, MACD, and Bollinger Bands.

3. **Set Parameters:** Define parameters for your indicators, such as lookback periods and threshold values. These parameters determine the algorithm's decision-making process.

4. **Risk Management:** Implement risk management measures, including stop-loss levels and position sizes, to control potential losses.

5. **Backtesting:** Backtest your algorithm using historical data to assess its performance under various market conditions. Ensure that the algorithm aligns with your trading objectives.

6. **Paper Trading:** Before deploying your algorithm in live markets, conduct paper trading to simulate real market conditions and evaluate its effectiveness.

7. **Optimization:** Continuously optimize your algorithm based on performance metrics and changing market conditions. Be cautious not to over-optimize, as this may lead to curve-fitting and poor future performance.

Risks and Considerations in Algorithmic Trading

While algorithmic trading offers numerous advantages, it comes with its own set of risks and considerations:

1. **Technical Failures:** Algorithmic trading systems are vulnerable to technical glitches, system failures, and connectivity issues, which can result in significant financial losses.

2. **Market Impact:** Large-scale algorithmic trading can impact market liquidity and lead to sudden price movements. This is known as "flash crashes" and can have widespread implications.

3. **Overfitting:** Over-optimizing algorithms for historical data (overfitting) may lead to poor performance in live markets due to a lack of adaptability to changing conditions.

4. **Regulatory Compliance:** Algorithmic traders must adhere to regulatory requirements and ensure that their systems comply with market regulations.

5. **Market Abuse:** Algorithmic trading can be susceptible to market manipulation, requiring vigilance to prevent unintended market abuse.

6. **Cybersecurity:** The reliance on technology makes algorithmic trading systems vulnerable to cybersecurity threats. Protecting against data breaches and hacking attempts is paramount.

In conclusion, algorithmic trading is a powerful tool for intraday traders seeking efficiency, precision, and speed in executing strategies. By understanding the basics, developing simple algorithms, and being mindful of the risks and considerations, traders can harness the benefits of algorithmic trading while mitigating potential pitfalls. As we progress through this guide, we will explore additional intraday trading strategies, each providing valuable insights and techniques for navigating the dynamic landscape of intraday trading.

CHAPTER 11

RISK MANAGEMENT TECHNIQUES

Effective risk management is a cornerstone of successful intraday trading. Traders must employ strategies to protect their capital and navigate the inherent uncertainties of financial markets. This chapter explores essential risk management techniques, including position sizing, setting stop-loss orders, and the importance of diversification in intraday trading.

Position Sizing

Position sizing is the process of determining the amount of capital to invest in a single trade. Proper position sizing helps control risk and prevents substantial losses that could negatively impact a trader's overall capital. Here's a guide to effective position sizing:

1. **Risk Per Trade:** Define a percentage of your trading capital that you are willing to risk on a single trade. A common rule of thumb is risking 1% to 3% of your total capital on any given trade.

2. **Volatility Considerations:** Adjust position sizes based on the volatility of the asset you are trading. More volatile instruments may require smaller position sizes to accommodate price fluctuations.

3. **Account Size:** The size of your trading account directly influences position sizing. Smaller accounts may necessitate more conservative position sizes to preserve capital.

4. **Trade Confidence:** Align position sizes with your confidence level in the trade. Higher-confidence trades may warrant larger positions, while lower-confidence trades may require smaller allocations.

5. **Correlation:** Consider the correlation between different trades in your portfolio. Avoid

overconcentration in a single asset or market, as this can increase overall risk.

Setting Stop-Loss Orders

A stop-loss order is a risk management tool designed to limit potential losses by automatically closing a position when the market reaches a predetermined price level. Here are key considerations for setting stop-loss orders:

1. **Percentage-Based Stops:** Set stop-loss orders based on a percentage of the asset's current price or the total amount you are willing to risk on the trade. This aligns with your predetermined risk per trade.

2. **Volatility-Adjusted Stops:** Adjust stop-loss levels based on the volatility of the asset. More volatile assets may require wider stop-loss levels to accommodate price fluctuations.

3. **Technical Levels:** Base stop-loss orders on key technical levels, such as support and resistance, trendlines, or moving averages. This ensures alignment with the technical structure of the market.

4. **Avoiding Round Numbers:** Consider placing stop-loss orders away from round numbers to reduce the likelihood of triggering stops due to market noise around these levels.

5. **Trailing Stops:** Use trailing stops to adjust stop-loss levels as the price moves in your favor. This allows you to capture profits while protecting against potential reversals.

Diversification in Intraday Trading

Diversification is a risk management technique that involves spreading investments across different assets or markets to reduce the impact of a poor-performing investment on the overall portfolio. In intraday trading, diversification can be applied in the following ways:

1. **Asset Classes:** Diversify across different asset classes, such as stocks, commodities, and currencies. Each asset class may respond differently to market conditions, providing balance in your portfolio.

2. **Sectors and Industries:** If trading stocks, consider diversifying across different sectors and industries. This helps mitigate the risk associated with poor performance in a specific sector.

3. **Timeframes:** Diversify intraday trading strategies across different timeframes. This can involve trading both shorter-term and longer-term trends to capture a range of market movements.

4. **Correlations:** Be mindful of the correlation between assets in your portfolio. Avoid overconcentration in

assets that are highly correlated, as this may increase overall portfolio risk.

5. **Number of Trades:** Diversify the number of trades in your portfolio to avoid overreliance on a small number of positions. A well-diversified portfolio can better withstand the impact of individual trade outcomes.

In conclusion, risk management is a critical aspect of intraday trading. By incorporating effective position sizing, setting disciplined stop-loss orders, and implementing diversification strategies, traders can mitigate risks and increase the likelihood of long-term success. As we progress through this guide, we will continue to explore additional intraday trading strategies and techniques to enhance your skills in navigating the dynamic landscape of intraday trading.

CHAPTER 12

PSYCHOLOGY OF INTRADAY TRADING

The psychology of intraday trading is a fundamental aspect that greatly influences a trader's success. Mastering the psychological aspects of trading is often as crucial as understanding market dynamics and employing effective strategies. This chapter delves into managing emotions, the importance of discipline and patience, and the valuable lessons to be gained from losses.

Managing Emotions

Intraday trading can be emotionally charged, with the potential for rapid market movements inducing stress, anxiety, and excitement. Effectively managing emotions is essential for making rational decisions and maintaining long-term success:

1. **Self-Awareness:** Recognize and acknowledge your emotions. Being aware of how you feel during trading can help you make more deliberate and rational decisions.

2. **Mindfulness:** Practice mindfulness techniques to stay focused on the present moment. This can prevent dwelling on past trades or worrying about future outcomes.

3. **Stress Reduction:** Implement stress reduction techniques, such as deep breathing, meditation, or exercise. Managing stress helps maintain emotional balance during intense trading periods.

4. **Set Realistic Expectations:** Establish realistic expectations for each trade and the overall performance of your trading strategy. Unrealistic expectations can lead to frustration and emotional distress.

5. **Take Breaks:** Step away from the screen during periods of heightened emotion. Taking short breaks can help reset your mindset and prevent impulsive decision-making.

Discipline and Patience

Discipline and patience are virtues that can significantly contribute to a trader's success. In the fast-paced environment of intraday trading, exercising discipline and practicing patience can make a substantial difference:

1. **Stick to Your Trading Plan:** Develop a well-thought-out trading plan and adhere to it. Discipline involves following your predetermined strategies and not deviating based on emotions or impulsive decisions.

2. **Avoid Overtrading:** Overtrading is a common pitfall in intraday trading. Discipline yourself to trade only when your predefined criteria are met, preventing unnecessary exposure to market risks.

3. **Wait for Ideal Setups:** Be patient and wait for high-probability setups. Avoid entering trades simply for the sake of being active. Patience allows you to select trades with the best risk-reward profiles.

4. **Learn to Accept Missed Opportunities:** Not every potential trade will align with your strategy or timing. Accepting missed opportunities is part of a disciplined

approach, preventing frustration and impulsive actions.

5. **Review and Reflect:** Regularly review your trades and reflect on your performance. Identify areas where discipline or patience may have wavered and work on improvement.

Learning from Losses

Losses are an inevitable part of trading, and approaching them as learning opportunities is crucial for personal and professional growth:

1. **Embrace Losses as Feedback:** View losses as feedback on your strategy rather than personal failures. Analyze losing trades objectively to identify areas for improvement.

2. **Keep a Trading Journal:** Maintain a detailed trading journal that includes not only your winning trades but also your losing ones. Record your thought process, emotions, and lessons learned.

3. **Adjust Your Approach:** Use insights gained from losses to adjust and refine your trading approach. Continuous improvement is key to adapting to changing market conditions.

4. **Focus on Process, Not Outcome:** Instead of fixating on individual trade outcomes, focus on the

consistency of your trading process. A solid process is more likely to yield positive results over the long term.

5. **Seek Support:** Discussing losses with fellow traders or seeking the guidance of a mentor can provide valuable perspectives and insights. Sharing experiences can help normalize setbacks and foster a positive mindset.

In conclusion, the psychology of intraday trading plays a pivotal role in a trader's overall success. By effectively managing emotions, practicing discipline and patience, and learning from losses, traders can cultivate a mindset conducive to making rational decisions and navigating the dynamic challenges of intraday trading. As we progress through this guide, we will continue to explore additional intraday trading strategies and techniques to enhance your skills in this demanding yet rewarding field.

CHAPTER 13

RECORD-KEEPING AND ANALYSIS

Record-keeping and analysis are indispensable components of a successful intraday trading journey. Maintaining a comprehensive trading journal, analyzing trade performance, and committing to continuous learning are key practices that contribute to a trader's growth and long-term success. This chapter explores the importance of keeping a trading journal, methods for analyzing trade performance, and the mindset of continuous learning and improvement.

Importance of Keeping a Trading Journal

A trading journal is a detailed record of a trader's activities, including executed trades, market observations, and emotional states during trading sessions. Here's why keeping a trading journal is crucial:

1. **Objective Assessment:** A trading journal provides an objective record of trades and decisions. This enables traders to analyze their performance without the influence of real-time emotions.

2. **Identifying Patterns:** Patterns and trends in your trading behavior become more apparent when documented over time. Recognizing recurring mistakes or successful strategies is vital for improvement.

3. **Emotional Awareness:** Recording emotions felt during trades enhances emotional awareness. Understanding how emotions impact decision-making helps in developing strategies to manage them effectively.

4. **Performance Evaluation:** A trading journal allows for a thorough evaluation of performance metrics,

including win-loss ratios, risk-reward ratios, and overall profitability.

5. **Reviewing Trading Plans:** Regularly reviewing your trading plan in the context of past trades helps ensure alignment with your objectives and can lead to necessary adjustments.

Analyzing Trade Performance

Analyzing trade performance involves scrutinizing past trades to identify strengths, weaknesses, and areas for improvement. Here are key aspects to consider during the analysis:

1. **Win-Loss Ratios:** Examine the ratio of winning to losing trades. A positive win-loss ratio is generally indicative of a successful strategy, but it's crucial to assess other metrics as well.

2. **Risk-Reward Ratios:** Evaluate the risk-reward ratios of trades. A favorable risk-reward ratio is essential for long-term profitability, as it ensures that potential gains outweigh potential losses.

3. **Consistency:** Assess the consistency of your trading approach. Consistency in executing your strategy and adhering to risk management rules contributes to stability and reliability.

4. **Identifying Patterns:** Look for patterns in your trading behavior and decision-making. Identifying patterns, whether positive or negative, enables targeted adjustments to your trading approach.

5. **Correlations with Market Conditions:** Analyze how your strategy performs under various market conditions. Understanding the environments in which your strategy thrives or struggles enhances adaptability.

Continuous Learning and Improvement

The pursuit of continuous learning is a hallmark of successful intraday traders. The financial markets are dynamic, and adapting to changing conditions is essential for long-term success. Here's how to foster a mindset of continuous learning and improvement:

1. **Post-Trade Reviews:** Conduct thorough post-trade reviews to extract lessons from each trade, regardless of outcome. Reflect on decisions, market conditions, and execution.

2. **Stay Informed:** Keep abreast of market news, economic events, and changes in market dynamics. Staying informed enables you to adapt your strategies to current conditions.

3. **Seek Feedback:** Engage with fellow traders, mentors, or trading communities to seek feedback and different perspectives. Constructive criticism and diverse insights contribute to growth.

4. **Experiment with New Strategies:** While consistency is crucial, being open to experimenting with new strategies or refining existing ones allows for evolution and adaptation to market changes.

5. **Professional Development:** Invest time in professional development. Attend workshops, webinars, and read relevant literature to stay informed about the latest trends and methodologies in trading.

In conclusion, record-keeping and analysis form the backbone of a trader's journey towards success. By maintaining a detailed trading journal, regularly analyzing trade performance, and fostering a mindset of continuous learning and improvement, traders can refine their skills, adapt to market changes, and enhance their overall performance in the dynamic world of intraday trading. As we conclude this guide, remember that the journey of an intraday trader is a continuous process of learning, adapting, and growing in response to the challenges and opportunities presented by the financial markets.

CHAPTER 14

PUTTING IT ALL TOGETHER - CREATING YOUR INTRADAY TRADING PLAN

Creating a well-defined intraday trading plan is the culmination of the knowledge, strategies, and skills acquired throughout this guide. In this chapter, we will explore the process of building a personalized trading plan, the importance of testing and adjusting strategies, and setting realistic goals for your intraday trading endeavors.

Building a Personalized Trading Plan

A personalized trading plan serves as a roadmap for your intraday trading activities. It incorporates elements such as risk management, strategies, and specific guidelines tailored to your trading style. Here's how to build a personalized trading plan:

1. **Define Your Trading Style:** Clarify whether you are a day trader, scalper, or a swing trader. Your trading style influences the timeframes you operate in and the strategies you employ.

2. **Risk Tolerance and Capital Allocation:** Establish your risk tolerance per trade and determine how much of your trading capital you are willing to risk. This is crucial for position sizing and overall risk management.

3. **Select Trading Strategies:** Choose the intraday trading strategies that align with your preferences, risk tolerance, and market conditions. Your strategies should be well-defined and tested.

4. **Set Clear Entry and Exit Criteria:** Define clear criteria for entering and exiting trades. This includes technical indicators, price levels, or other factors that trigger trade execution and closure.

5. **Incorporate Risk Management:** Integrate risk management techniques, including stop-loss orders and position sizing, into your plan. Ensure that your risk per trade aligns with your overall risk tolerance.

6. **Develop a Routine:** Create a daily routine that encompasses pre-market analysis, strategy selection, and post-market review. Consistency in your routine helps reinforce discipline.

7. **Review and Adjust:** Regularly review and adjust your trading plan based on your evolving experience, market conditions, and changes in your risk profile.

Testing and Adjusting Strategies

Testing and adjusting your intraday trading strategies are vital steps in optimizing your plan for real-world market conditions. Here's how to approach this process:

1. **Backtesting:** Use historical data to backtest your strategies. Evaluate how well they would have performed in past market conditions. This provides insights into potential strengths and weaknesses.

2. **Paper Trading:** Conduct paper trading or simulated trading to test your strategies in real-time conditions without risking actual capital. This helps validate your strategies and familiarizes you with their execution.

3. **Evaluate Results:** Assess the results of your backtesting and paper trading. Identify patterns, measure performance metrics, and gain a comprehensive understanding of how your strategies perform.

4. **Adjust Parameters:** If necessary, adjust parameters of your strategies based on your evaluation. This may involve refining entry and exit criteria, optimizing indicators, or modifying risk management rules.

5. **Learn from Mistakes:** Embrace mistakes and losses as learning opportunities. Analyze unsuccessful trades to understand what went wrong and use these insights to enhance your strategies.

Setting Realistic Goals

Setting realistic goals is a critical aspect of managing expectations and measuring success in intraday trading. Here's how to establish achievable and meaningful goals:

1. **Financial Objectives:** Define specific financial goals, such as daily, weekly, or monthly profit targets.

Ensure these targets are realistic and in alignment with your risk tolerance and capital.

2. **Performance Metrics:** Establish performance metrics that go beyond profit and loss. Consider metrics like win-loss ratios, risk-reward ratios, and consistency in following your trading plan.

3. **Learning Goals:** Include learning goals in your plan. These might involve acquiring new skills, understanding different strategies, or staying updated on market developments.

4. **Adaptability:** Recognize the dynamic nature of financial markets. Set goals that allow for adaptability to changing market conditions, strategies, and personal development.

5. **Evaluate and Adjust Goals:** Regularly evaluate your progress toward your goals. If necessary, adjust them based on your evolving experience, achievements, and challenges encountered.

In conclusion, creating your intraday trading plan involves a thoughtful integration of strategies, risk management, and personal goals. By building a personalized plan, testing and adjusting your strategies, and setting realistic goals, you lay the foundation for a sustainable and successful intraday trading journey. Remember that intraday trading is not only about generating profits but also about continuous learning, adaptability, and the pursuit of excellence in navigating the dynamic landscape of financial markets.

CHAPTER 15

ADVANCED INTRADAY TRADING TECHNIQUES

As you progress in your intraday trading journey, exploring advanced techniques becomes essential to adapt to diverse market conditions and capitalize on unique opportunities. This chapter delves into advanced intraday trading techniques, including options trading strategies, navigating economic events, and considerations for trading in the global market.

Options Trading Strategies

Options trading provides advanced traders with additional tools for expressing market views and managing risk. Incorporating options into your intraday trading strategies can enhance flexibility and offer unique advantages. Here are key options trading strategies for intraday traders:

1. **Day Trading Options:** Execute options trades with a short-term perspective, capitalizing on intraday price movements. Day trading options can involve both calls and puts, depending on market expectations.

2. **Straddle and Strangle:** Use a straddle or strangle strategy when anticipating significant price volatility. A straddle involves simultaneously buying a call and a put with the same strike price, while a strangle involves buying options with different strike prices.

3. **Iron Condor:** Deploy an iron condor strategy to profit from low volatility. This involves simultaneously selling an out-of-the-money call and put while buying

further out-of-the-money call and put options to limit potential losses.

4. **Credit and Debit Spreads:** Employ credit spreads, such as bull put spreads or bear call spreads, to generate premium income while managing risk. Alternatively, use debit spreads, like bull call spreads or bear put spreads, to achieve directional exposure with limited risk.

5. **Gamma Scalping:** Gamma scalping involves actively adjusting options positions to exploit changes in the underlying asset's price. Traders engage in gamma scalping to profit from short-term price fluctuations.

Trading during Economic Events

Economic events, such as central bank announcements, employment reports, and GDP releases, can trigger significant market volatility. Incorporating strategies to navigate these events is crucial for advanced intraday traders:

1. **Event Calendar Awareness:** Stay informed about economic events through an economic calendar. Mark key events that may impact the instruments you trade.

2. **Preparation and Scenario Analysis:** Before an economic event, conduct thorough analysis and

scenario planning. Anticipate potential market reactions based on different outcomes.

3. **Volatility Strategies:** Adjust position sizes and risk management parameters to account for increased volatility during and after economic events. Consider using options strategies to hedge against unexpected price movements.

4. **Fast Execution:** Be prepared to execute trades swiftly as soon as the market reacts to economic news. Rapid decision-making is crucial to capitalize on short-lived opportunities.

5. **Post-Event Analysis:** Review your trades and performance after economic events. Evaluate the effectiveness of your strategies and identify areas for improvement in handling similar events in the future.

Global Market Considerations

Intraday traders often have access to a variety of global markets. Understanding how to navigate these markets enhances the scope of trading opportunities. Consider the following global market considerations:

1. **Time Zone Awareness:** Be aware of different market opening and closing times around the world. Optimize your trading schedule to align with peak liquidity periods.

2. **Currency Pairs:** Trade currency pairs that align with your intraday strategy. Major currency pairs, such as EUR/USD or USD/JPY, are often more liquid and offer tighter spreads.

3. **Cross-Market Correlations:** Understand correlations between different asset classes and markets. Changes in one market may impact another, providing opportunities for cross-market trades.

4. **News Flow:** Stay informed about global news and events that could impact various markets. Develop strategies that consider the interconnectedness of global financial markets.

5. **Market Accessibility:** Leverage technology to access global markets efficiently. Electronic trading platforms and direct market access (DMA) enable intraday traders to execute trades across different exchanges.

In conclusion, mastering advanced intraday trading techniques involves incorporating options strategies, navigating economic events, and considering the dynamics of global markets. As you integrate these advanced techniques into your trading repertoire, continue to emphasize risk management, discipline, and continuous learning. The ability to adapt to diverse market conditions is key to sustained success in the dynamic world of intraday trading.

CONCLUSION

MASTERING THE ART OF INTRADAY TRADING

Embarking on the journey of mastering intraday trading requires a combination of knowledge, discipline, and adaptability. In this comprehensive guide, we have covered a spectrum of topics, from the fundamentals of intraday trading to advanced techniques. Whether you are a novice or an experienced trader, the principles explored here provide a foundation for navigating the dynamic landscape of intraday trading.

Key takeaways from this guide include:

1. **Understanding Market Dynamics:** Grasp the fundamental principles that drive financial markets, including market participants, order types, and the impact of macroeconomic factors.

2. **Intraday Trading Strategies:** Explore a variety of intraday trading strategies, including momentum trading, gap trading, breakout trading, reversal trading, scalping, mean reversion trading, and algorithmic trading.

3. **Risk Management Techniques:** Implement effective risk management strategies, such as position sizing, setting stop-loss orders, and diversification, to protect your capital and mitigate potential losses.

4. **Psychology of Trading:** Mastering the psychology of intraday trading is crucial for success. Learn to manage emotions, exercise discipline, and embrace continuous learning and improvement.

5. **Record-Keeping and Analysis:** Maintain a detailed trading journal, analyze trade performance, and

commit to continuous learning to refine your skills and adapt to changing market conditions.

6. **Creating a Trading Plan:** Develop a personalized intraday trading plan that aligns with your trading style, risk tolerance, and goals. Regularly test and adjust strategies to optimize performance.

7. **Advanced Techniques:** Explore advanced intraday trading techniques, including options trading strategies, navigating economic events, and considerations for trading in the global market.

As you progress on your intraday trading journey, remember that success is a continuous process of adaptation, learning, and refinement. Stay disciplined, manage risks effectively, and remain open to evolving your strategies in response to market dynamics.

APPENDIX

RESOURCES FOR INTRADAY TRADERS

To further enhance your intraday trading skills, consider exploring additional resources, including recommended books, online courses, and trading communities.

Recommended Books:

1. "A Random Walk Down Wall Street" by Burton G. Malkiel

2. "Reminiscences of a Stock Operator" by Edwin Lefèvre

3. "Market Wizards" by Jack D. Schwager

4. "Technical Analysis of the Financial Markets" by John J. Murphy

5. "Flash Boys" by Michael Lewis

Online Courses:

1. Investopedia Academy - Become a Day Trader

2. Coursera - Financial Markets and Investment Strategy

3. Udemy - Intraday Trading for Beginners

Trading Communities:

1. Elite Trader Forum

2. Trade2Win Forum

3. Reddit - Day Trading Community

These resources provide additional insights, perspectives, and opportunities for learning from experienced traders. Engaging with these materials and communities can contribute to your growth as an intraday trader.

Lalit Prasad Mohanty

Lalit Prasad Mohanty

Lalit Prasad Mohanty

Lalit Prasad Mohanty

Lalit Prasad Mohanty

Lalit Prasad Mohanty

www.ingramcontent.com/pod-product-compliance
Lightning Source LLC
Chambersburg PA
CBHW062356290526
45794CB00005B/2256